HORRID HENRY'S HILARIOUSLY HORRID JOKE BOOK

Francesca Simon spent her childhood on the beach in California, and then went to Yale and Oxford Universities to study medieval history and literature. She now lives in London with her English husband and their son. When she is not writing books she is chasing after her Tibetan Spaniel, Shanti.

Tony Ross is one of Britain's best known illustrators, with many picture books to his name as well as line drawings for many fiction titles. He lives in Oxfordshire.

HORRID HENRY'S HILARIOUSLY HORRID JOKE BOOK

Francesca Simon

Illustrated by Tony Ross

Orion
Children's Books

First published in Great Britain in 2010
by Orion Children's Books
a division of the Orion Publishing Group Ltd
Orion House
5 Upper Saint Martin's Lane
London WC2H 9EA
An Hachette UK Company

1 3 5 7 9 10 8 6 4 2

The Orion Publishing Group's policy is to use papers
that are natural, renewable and recyclable products and
made from wood grown in sustainable forests. The logging
and manufacturing processes are expected to conform to
the environmental regulations of the country of origin.

ISBN 978 1 4440 0087 0

CONTENTS

HORRID HENRY'S HILARIOUSLY HORRID JOKE BOOK

Phew. I'm exhausted. Instead of spending Christmas lounging on the comfy black chair eating Belcher Squelchers and watching Knight Fight, I've been writing my best joke book yet. I've got 365 extra special, super-duper fantastically funny jokes, one for every single day of the year. Anyway, Happy New Year everyone. Except of course, Peter. And Margaret. And Steve. And Bill. And Rebecca. Nasty New Year to all my evil enemies. But a great one to Purple Hand Gang members everywhere!

HAPPY NEW YEAR

Knock, knock!
Who's there?
Happy.
Happy who?
Happy New Year!

What do
vampires sing
on New Year's Eve?
Old Fang Syne.

What's a cow's favourite
day of the year?
MOO Year's Day!

And what's a cat's favourite day?
MEW Year's Day!

GRUMPY NEXT-DOOR NEIGHBOUR:
Didn't you hear me banging on your wall last night?
HAPPY NEXT-DOOR NEIGHBOUR:
Oh, don't worry about it. We had a New Year's Eve party and made lots of noise too.

Where does Tarzan buy his clothes?
At a jungle sale.

How many months have twenty-eight days?
All of them.

How many seconds are there in a year?
Twelve. The 2nd of January, the 2nd of February, the 2nd of March...

JOLLY JOKES
TO START
THE YEAR

What occurs once in a minute, twice in a moment, but never in an hour? The letter 'm'.

What do you take the top off to put the bottom on? A toilet seat.

What do you call a dinosaur with only one eye? A Do-you-think-he-saw-us.

What do you call a dinosaur that changes its mind? A Now-I'm-not-so-sure-us.

How do you know when there's
an elephant under your bed?
Your nose touches the ceiling.

Why is getting up at six o'clock in
the morning like a pig's tail?
It's twirly!

Why was the mermaid thrown out of the choir?
She couldn't carry a tuna.

What do you get when you cross
a knight with a mosquito?
A bite in shining armour.

Why is the sky so high?
So that birds won't bump their heads.

*What's the difference between
a unicorn and a lettuce?*
One's a funny beast and
the other's a bunny feast.

How do you fix a tuba?
With a tuba glue.

*What did the Sheriff
of Nottingham say
when Robin Hood
fired at him and
missed?*

That was an-arrow
escape.

FEBRUARY FUN

**Yay! February's my birthday.
Line up, line up, lots of presents
needed!**

Why did Lazy Linda go to bed early?
Because she was feeling Febru-weary.

*What did the boy squirrel say to the girl
squirrel on Valentine's Day?*
I'm nuts about you!

*What did the girl squirrel say
to the boy squirrel?*
You're nuts so bad yourself!

*What did the ram say to his girlfriend
on Valentine's Day?*
I love ewe.

*What did the caveman give his girlfriend on
Valentine's Day?*
Ugs and kisses.

Why did the acrobats get married?
They were head over heels in love.

What do you call a very small Valentine?
A Valentiny!

Roses are red, violets are blue,
Most poems rhyme,
But this one doesn't.
Tee hee!

What's green and only comes out
on February 29th?
A leapfrog.

BIRTHDAY BELLY-LAUGHS

What's a camel's favourite party game?
Musical Humps.

What's a cow's favourite party game?
Moosical Chairs.

What do you say to a cow on its birthday?
Happy birthday to moo.

That one's for you, Maggie Moo Moo.

Don't call me that!

Call you what, Moo Moo?

What do you say to a cat on its birthday?
Happy birthday to mew.

*What do you say to a parrot
on its birthday?*
Happy birdy to you.

What do you get every birthday?
A year older.

TOUGH TOBY: Henry, when is
your birthday?
HORRID HENRY: Every year!

What's the best birthday present in the world?
A broken drum, you can't beat it!

KNOCK, KNOCK! SPRING'S HERE

(About time, too.)

Knock, knock!
Who's there?
Woo.
Woo, who?
Calm down, it's just a joke.

Knock, knock!
Who's there?
A little old man.
A little old man who?
A little old man who can't reach the doorbell.

Knock, knock!
Who's there?
Let us.
Let us who?
Let us in and you'll soon find out.

Knock, knock!
Who's there?
Dishes.
Dishes who?
Dishes me.
Who ish you?

Knock, knock!
Who's there?
Gorilla.
Gorilla who?
Gorilla me some cheese on toast, I'm hungry.

Knock, knock!
Who's there?
Tank!
Tank who?
You're welcome!

SPRING

whoopee

Spring. Birds tweeting.
Trees budding.
Butterflies flapping.
Yeah, who cares, right?
Spring means April Fools' Day!
And great jokes to annoy little
brothers and sisters!
And loads and loads and loads
of chocolate for Easter!

SPRING SIDESPLITTERS

Knock, knock!
Who's there?
Cook.
Cook who?
That's the first cuckoo I've heard this year.

What's green and jumps around the garden?
A spring onion.

*Why did the hen leap over
the road?*
She was a spring chicken.

Can February March?
No, but April May!

What colour is the wind?
Blew.

Why is everyone tired on April 1st?
Because they've just finished a 31-day March.

*When's the best time to go
on a trampoline?*
Spring!

How does Peter frog feel when he has a broken leg?
Very unhoppy.

Mum! Henry called me a frog!

How do you make a butterfly?
Flick it out of the dish with a butter knife.

*What do you call the snail
that crossed the road?*
Lucky.

*What did the mother worm
say to the baby worm?*
Where in earth have
you been?

What's green and sits in the corner?
A naughty frog.

**A naughty frog-face named Peter
- tee hee!**

Mum!

RAINY
RIBTICKLERS

*Who designed the first
rain jacket?*
Anna Rack.

*What goes up when
the rain comes down?*
An umbrella.

What do Jelly Babies wear in the rain?
Gum boots.

What's the difference between a wet day and a lion with toothache?
One's pouring with rain; the other's roaring with pain.

When should a mouse carry an umbrella?
When it's raining cats and dogs.

What do owls sing when it's raining?
Too wet to woo.

PONGY PETS

Why did the man buy all the birds
at the pet shop?
They were going
cheep.

MUM: Have you given the goldfish
their fresh water?
LAZY LINDA: No, they haven't
drunk the water I gave them last
week yet.

Moody Margaret saw Horrid Henry
with a newt on his shoulder.
"What do you call him?" asked
Moody Margaret.
"Tiny," said Horrid Henry.
"Why do you call him Tiny?"
"Because he's my newt!"

PATIENT: Doctor! Doctor!
I think I need glasses.
DOCTOR: I think you're right.
This is a pet shop!

What do you call a really happy rodent?
A grinny pig.

*What did the dog say when he sat on the
sandpaper?*
Rough, rough.

Where do you find a birthday present for a cat?
In a cat-alogue.

NEW NICK: I play scrabble
with my dog every night.
BRAINY BRIAN:
He must be clever.
NEW NICK:
I don't know about
that. I usually beat him.

*When is it bad to have a black cat
following you?*
When you're a mouse.

What do you say to a miserable budgie?
Chirrup.

APRIL FOOLS' DAY FUN

On April Fools' Day, what goes "He he, bonk"?
Horrid Henry laughing his head off.

Do you know what happens on April 1st?
Yes, I'm fooly aware of it!

What would you get if you crossed April 1st with Halloween?
April Ghouls' Day.

HORRID HENRY: If a red house is made of red bricks, and a blue house is made of blue bricks, what's a green house made of?

PERFECT PETER: Green bricks, of course.

HORRID HENRY: Fooled you! It's made of GLASS!

Peter is a frog, Peter is a frog!

Muuuuuum! Henry's being horrid.

Don't be horrid, Henry!

RUDE RALPH: What's green and purple, with googly eyes and big sharp teeth?

HORRID HENRY: I don't know. Why?

RUDE RALPH: Because one's just climbing up your leg!

Knock, knock!
Who's there?
Twitter.
Twitter who?
Ha ha! You sound just like an owl!

Will you remember me tomorrow?
Yes.
Will you remember me next week?
Yes.
Will you remember me next month?
Yes.
Will you remember me next year?
Yes.
Knock, knock!
Who's there?
April Fools! You've forgotten me already!

RUDE RALPH: I'm so thirsty
mymy tongue's hanging out.
MOODY MARGARET: Is that
your tongue? It looks like a horrible
spotted tie.

Peter, what's
frozen water?
It's ice, Henry.
What's frozen
cream?

That's easy, ice-cream.
What about frozen tea?
Iced tea.
And frozen ink?
Iced ink.
Ha ha, Peter! April Fools -
you'd better have a bath then!
Mum! Henry said I stink!
Did not!
Did too!

MUM: Why have you been sent home from school early?

HORRID HENRY: I set fire to something in cookery class.

MUM: Oh dear! What was it?

HORRID HENRY: The school! ....Ha ha! April Fools!

HORRID HENRY: Why have you got a sausage behind your ear?

MISS BATTLE-AXE: Oh no, I must have eaten my pencil for lunch!

HORRID HENRY: April Fools!

What do you have in April that you don't have in any other month?
The letter 'i'!

How do you make Beefy Bert laugh on April Fools' Day?
Tell him a joke on the 31st March.

HORRID HENRY: What sort of candle burns longer?
MUM: Mm… I'll have to think carefully about that one.
HORRID HENRY: April Fools! They all burn SHORTER!

HORRID HENRY:
Dad, have you heard the latest newsflash? A 4-foot man and a 9-foot woman have just escaped from prison. The police are looking HIGH and LOW for them – tee hee!

FUNNY FARMYARDS

What do you call a donkey with only three legs?
A wonkey.

What do you call a cow eating grass?
A lawn moo-er.

What do you call a pony with a sore throat?
A little horse.

What do you get when you cross a chicken with a thief?
A peck-pocket.

*Did you know it takes three sheep
to make a sweater?*
I didn't even know they could knit!

What kind of tie does a pig wear?
A pig-sty.

1ST COW: Have you heard about
this mad cow disease?
2ND COW: Don't ask me, I'm a
buttercup!

What goes moo, baa, oink, woof, quack?
A cow that can speak five languages.

BEASTLY LITTLE BROTHER AND STINKY LITTLE SISTER JOKES

MUM: I'm going to the doctor's. I don't like the look of your little brother.
HORRID HENRY: I'll come with you. I don't like the look of him either.

Does your little brother keep himself clean?
Oh yes. He takes a bath every month whether he needs one or not.

LISPY LILY: Shall I put the telly on?
NEW NICK: It might look better than that dress you're wearing.

HORRID HENRY: Why are you sitting in the rabbit's cage?

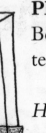

PERFECT PETER: Because I want to be the teacher's pet.

How many little brothers and sisters does it take to do the washing-up after lunch?
Three – one to wash, one to dry and one to pick up the pieces.

DAD: What's on the telly tonight?
PERFECT PETER: Same as always, Dad, a vase of flowers and a picture of Grandma.

What happens when your little sister falls down on the ice?
She gets thaw.

How many little brothers and sisters does it take to change a light bulb?
Ten! One to change the light bulb and nine to stand on each other's shoulders!

EASTER WISECRACKS

*Why did the boiled egg
win the race?*
It couldn't be beaten.

*Why shouldn't you tell
an Easter egg a joke?*
It might crack up.

What did one Easter egg say to the other?
Got any good yolks.

How do rabbits stay fit?
EGG-xercise and HARE-robics!

*What do you call a rabbit that
tells good jokes?*
A funny bunny!

Why do we paint eggs at Easter?
Because it's easier than trying to
wallpaper them.

Why did the egg go into the jungle?
Because it was an EGG-splorer.

*What do you call a chick that
wears a shellsuit?*
An egg!

KNOCK, KNOCK! LET IN THE SUMMER

Race you to the Frosty-Freeze ice cream factory!

Knock, knock!
Who's there?
Luck.
Luck who?
Luck through the keyhole and you'll find out.

Knock, knock!
Who's there?
Wooden shoe.
Wooden shoe who?
Wooden shoe like to know?

Knock, knock!
Who's there?
Atch.
Atch who?
Bless you!

Knock, knock!
Who's there?
Ya.
Ya who?
I didn't know you were a cowboy!

Knock, knock!
Who's there?
Felix.
Felix who?
*Felix my ice-cream,
I'll lick his.*

Knock, knock!
Who's there?
Cash.
Cash who?
I knew you were nuts.

36

SUMMER

Summer! At last! Throw away those school books! No more carrot nose Miss Battle-Axe! No more tests! No more fractions! Now it's just fun fun fun. And loads of ice cream and lying in the sun blasting out The Killer Boy Rats and playing video games and – go away, Peter. I'm busy.

Henry, won't you play with me?

NO!

SPORTING GAGS

SUSAN: Mum, Miss Battle-Axe says I need new trainers for gym.
MUM: Well, tell her Jim will have to buy his own trainers.

Why doesn't the centipede get picked for the football team?
It takes him hours to get his boots on.

Horrid Henry missed a shot at goal, and the other team won. "I could kick myself," he moaned. "Don't bother," said Moody Margaret, "you'd miss!"

MOODY MARGARET: I'm sorry I'm late for school, Miss, but I was dreaming about football.

MISS BATTLE-AXE: Why does dreaming about football make you late for school?

MOODY MARGARET: They played extra time.

What smells horrible, runs about all day and lies around at night with its tongue hanging out?
One of Aerobic Al's old trainers.

What's the best way to win a race?
Run faster than everyone else!

HENRY'S DAD: Henry has got into the football team.
AL'S DAD: What position does he play?
HENRY'S DAD: He's left back in the changing room.

Twenty-two ants were playing football in a saucer. One ant says to the other, "We'll have to play better than this tomorrow – we're playing in the cup."

HORRID HOLIDAY HOWLERS

Who on the beach has the biggest sunhat?
The person with
the biggest head.

What do witches use in the summer?
Suntan potion.

Why was Greedy Graham doing the backstroke after lunch?
Because you're not supposed to swim on a full stomach.

*Why didn't Beefy Bert enjoy
his water skiing holiday?*
He couldn't find a sloping lake.

HENRY'S DAD: Are
the rooms here quiet?
HOTEL MANAGER:
Yes, sir, it's only the guests
that are noisy.

HENRY'S MUM: How much
do you charge for a week's stay?
HOTEL MANAGER: I don't know,
no one's ever stayed that long.

ANXIOUS ANDREW:
Do these ships sink often?
CAPTAIN: No, only once.

GLOBE-TROTTING GIGGLES

What's a volcano?
A mountain with hiccups.

What makes the Tower of Pisa lean?
It doesn't eat much.

Which country has the thinnest people?
Finland.

What's the coldest country in the world?
Chile.

What's the coldest city in Germany?
Brrrr-lin.

Where do sheep go on holiday?
The Baa-hamas.

What stays in one corner, but can go all around the world?
A postage stamp.

Where do elephants go on holiday?
Tuscany.

Where do cows go on holiday?
Moo Zealand.

Henry!
Stop saying 'Moo'.

OK, Maggie
Moo Moo.

Don't call
me that!

Where do cats go on holiday?
The Canary Islands.

ANIMALS IN THE SUN

Why did the monkey lie on the sunbed?
To get an orangu-tan.

What's grey, has four legs and a trunk?
A mouse going on holiday.

What's brown, has four legs and a trunk?
A mouse coming back from holiday.

*What do you get when you cross
an elephant with a fish?*
Swimming trunks.

What do bees say in summer?
'Swarm.

Why aren't elephants allowed on the beach?
In case their trunks fall down.

Where would you weigh a whale?
At a whale-weigh station.

*Why did the crab
go to jail?*
He kept pinching
things.

How did the frog cross the Channel?
By hoppercraft.

*What do horses suffer from in the
summertime?*
Neigh fever.

HAIRY HUMOUR

PATIENT: Doctor, doctor, my hair's coming out. Can you give me something to keep it in?
DOCTOR: Certainly – how about a plastic bag?

Why did Beefy Bert take his comb to the dentist?
Because its teeth were falling out.

PATIENT: Doctor, doctor, I keep thinking I'm a dog.
DOCTOR: Lie down on this couch and I'll examine you.
PATIENT: I'm not allowed. I might make it all hairy!

BARBER: How would you like your hair cut, sir?

MR MOSSY: Could you leave one side long and cut one side short, with a crooked fringe at the front and bald patches on the top?

BARBER: Oh dear, I don't think I can manage that, sir.

MR MOSSY: Why not? You did last time.

PATIENT: Doctor, doctor, my hair seems to be getting thinner.

DOCTOR: Why do you want fat hair?

Who can shave twenty-five times a day and still have a beard?
A barber.

Three men fall out of a boat but only two get their hair wet. Why?
Because the third man is bald!

SIZZLING SNACKS

What is a meatball?
A dance in the
butcher's shop.

How do you make a really good milkshake?
Tell it a scary story.

*What do you call a banana split
when you've dropped it from
the top of a skyscraper on to
the pavement below?*

A banana splat.

What do sheep enjoy on a sunny day?
Having a baa-becue.

How do monkeys toast bread?
They put it under the gorilla.

RICH AUNT RUBY:
Excuse me, waiter, is
there spaghetti on
the menu?
WAITER: No,
madam, I wiped
it off.

Why can't you starve in the desert?
Because of the sand which is there.

Have you ever seen a man-eating tiger?
No, but I've seen a man eating chicken.

Greedy Graham walked into a library, and
said to the librarian, "Cod and chips, please."
"This isn't a fish and chip shop," said the
librarian. "It's a library."
"Cod and chips, please," whispered
Greedy Graham.

FAMILY FUNNIES

MOODY MARGARET: I'm homesick.
MUM: But this is your home.
MOODY MARGARET: I know, and I'm sick of it.

My dad just opened a sweet shop.
I bet he makes a mint.

Did you hear about the well-behaved little boy? Whenever he was good, his dad gave him 10p and a pat on the head. By the time he was sixteen, he had £786 and a flat head.

WEEPY WILLIAM:
Do you notice any change
in me?
MUM: No. Why?
WEEPY WILLIAM:
I just swallowed 5p. Waaaa!

Daddy, there's a man
with a beard at the door.
DAD: Tell him I've got one already!

DAD: Who broke this
window?
HORRID HENRY:
It was Peter, Dad. I
threw an apple at him
and he ducked.

HORRID HENRY: Dad, could
you do my homework for me?
DAD: No, it wouldn't be right.
HORRID HENRY: But you
could at least try.

ZANY ZOOS AND BIZARRE BEASTS

What has an elephant's trunk, a lion's mane and a baboon's bottom?
A zoo.

What's black and white and red all over?
A shy zebra.

Where do baby apes sleep?
In apricots.

What kind of bird can write?
A PENguin.

Why didn't the viper
viper nose?
Because the adder
adder handkerchief.

What's long and green and goes hith?
A snake with a lisp.

GRIZZLY BEAR: Could I have a
lemonade.......and a chocolate muffin?
WAITRESS: Why the big pause?
GRIZZLY BEAR: I don't know.
My father had them too.

Why does a hummingbird hum?
It doesn't know the words.

What do you give a gorilla for his birthday?
I don't know, but let's hope he likes it!

What do you call a camel with three humps?
Humphrey.

What do you call a camel with no humps?
A horse.

Why didn't the old lady run away from the lion?
She knew it was a man-eater.

Why couldn't the leopard escape from the zoo?
It was always spotted.

What sort of ape can fly?
A hot air baboon.

What animal are you like when you have a bath?
A bear!

55

KNOCK, KNOCK! AUTUMN'S ON ITS WAY

Knock, knock!
Who's there?
You.
You who?
Did you call?

Knock, knock!
Who's there?
Dishes.
Dishes who?
Dishes a very bad joke.

Knock, knock!
Who's there?
Repeat.
Repeat who?
Who, who, who!

Knock, knock!
Who's there?
Cow-go.
Cow-go who?
No, cow go MOO!

Knock, knock!
Who's there?
Europe.
Europe who?
Europe up early for a lazybones.

Knock, knock!
Who's there?
Ralph.
Ralph who?
Ralph, Ralph – I'm just a puppy.

AUTUMN

Oh no!
It's so unfair!
Autumn means ...
school.
Aaarrrggghhhh.
Grisly grub school dinners and
spelling tests and Miss Battle-Axe
and her evil eye and big yellow
teeth and pointy fingers. Eeeek.

Well, let all my great jokes
cheer you up. Your teacher will
be putty in your hands once
you've learned my Horrible
History Howlers or my amazing
Ghostly Giggles.

And don't forget, autumn means
Halloween and loads and loads
and loads of sweets! Yippee!
Chocolate Hairballs here I come!

AUTUMN ANTICS

*Why do spiders like
the Internet?*
Because of all
the websites.

*What do you call a man who walks
through autumn leaves?*
Russell.

How does an elephant get down from a tree?
He sits on a leaf and waits for autumn.

*What's the best way to make a fire
using two sticks?*
Make sure one of them is a match!

What do you call a jacket that's on fire?
A blazer.

What did one autumn leaf say to the other?
I'm falling for you.

How do you mend a broken pumpkin?
With a pumpkin patch.

PERFECT PETER:
Am I too late for the
bonfire?
HORRID HENRY:
No, just jump up on
the sticks. There's
room next to that guy.

*What do you get if you
cross a dinosaur with a
firework?*
A dino-mite.

*Why did Beefy Bert hurt himself raking up
leaves?*
He fell out of the tree.

BACK TO SCHOOL

Boo - hiss!

SOUR SUSAN: What shall we play today?
MOODY MARGARET: Let's play school. I'll be the teacher.
SOUR SUSAN: OK! And I'll be absent!

What's Moody Margaret's favourite day of the week?
Moanday.

Why did the jellybean go to school?
Because he wanted to be a Smartie.

Why did the boy take a ladder to school?
Because it was a high school.

61

Why did the headmaster marry the school cleaner?
She swept him off his feet.

What was the blackbird doing in the school library?
Looking for bookworms.

What do you call an ant who skips school?
A tru-ant.

ANXIOUS ANDREW: I keep thinking I'm the school bell.
NURSE NEEDLE: Take these tablets and if they don't help, give me a ring in the morning.

Why did the boy take his car to school?
To drive his teacher up the wall.

What's the difference between Miss Battle-Axe and a steam train?
One says, "Spit out that chewing gum," and the other says, "Choo-choo!"

MR NERDON:
Ralph, don't hum while you're working.
RUDE RALPH: I'm not working, Sir, just humming.

SCHOOL GRUB GROSS-OUT

RUDE RALPH: How do you think they keep flies out of the school canteen?

HORRID HENRY: They probably let them taste the food!

MOODY MARGARET: Oh good, we're having salad for school dinner today.

SOUR SUSAN: How do you know it's salad?

MOODY MARGARET: Well, I can't smell anything burning.

GREEDY GRAHAM: I'm doing really well at school.

MUM: That's wonderful.

GREEDY GRAHAM: Yes, today I was first in the dinner queue.

What's a mushroom?
The place where they keep the school dinners.

GREEDY GRAHAM: Why is there a button in my lunch?

GREASY GRETA: It's off the jacket potatoes.

COOKERY TEACHER: Graham, what are the best things to put in a pie?

GREEDY GRAHAM: Teeth!

TERRIBLE TEACHER JOKES

What did the teacher say to the naughty bee?
Bee-hive yourself.

What are the only two good things about being a teacher?
MISS BATTLE-AXE: July and August.

MISS BATTLE-AXE: We call you "the wonder child" in the staff room.
RUDE RALPH: Why's that?
MISS BATTLE-AXE: Because we all wonder when you're going to wash!

MR NERDON: Henry, you're late for school again. What is it this time?

HORRID HENRY: I sprained my ankle, Sir.

MR NERDON: What a lame excuse!

MRS ODDBOD AT ASSEMBLY: Last night someone broke into the school stationery cupboard and stole a load of blunt pencils. The police described the theft as pointless.

What's the worst school trip?
The trip to the headteacher's office.

Why did the teacher wear dark glasses?
Because she had such a bright class.

What do you get when you cross a teacher with a vampire?
Lots of blood tests.

CLASSROOM CORNER

MISS BATTLE-AXE: What's the most important thing to remember in a chemistry lesson?
GREEDY GRAHAM: Don't lick the spoon.

MISS BATTLE-AXE: Henry, didn't you hear me call you?
HORRID HENRY: Yes, but you're always telling us not to answer back.

MUM: What did you learn at school today?
HORRID HENRY: Not enough.
I have to go back tomorrow.

MUM: I told you not to eat cake before supper.

GREEDY GRAHAM: But Mum, I'm just doing my Maths homework. If you take an eighth of a cake from a whole cake, how much is left?

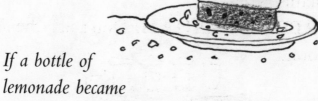

If a bottle of lemonade became a teacher, what subject would it teach? Fizzical education.

MISS BATTLE-AXE: Can anyone name a bird that doesn't build its own nest?

DIZZY DAVE: The cuckoo.

MISS BATTLE-AXE: That's right! How did you know that?

DIZZY DAVE: Because cuckoos live in clocks.

WORDY WHEEZES

MISS BATTLE-AXE: What does the word 'abundance' mean?

GREEDY GRAHAM: Lots of dancing cakes?

MISS BATTLE-AXE: Bert, what do we call the outside of a tree?

BEEFY BERT: I dunno, Miss.

MISS BATTLE-AXE: Bark, you silly boy, bark!

BEEFY BERT: Woof woof!

MISS BATTLE-AXE: Who can tell me what a cartoon is?

SINGING SORAYA: A song you sing in a car?

MISS LOVELY:
What's the plural of mouse?
TIDY TED: Mice.
MISS LOVELY:
What's the plural of baby?
TIDY TED: Twins.

MISS BATTLE-AXE:
Graham, what is 'can't' short for?
GREEDY GRAHAM:
Cannot.
MISS BATTLE-AXE:
And what is "don't"
short for?
GREEDY GRAHAM:
Doughnut!

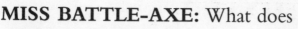

MISS BATTLE-AXE: What does
minimum mean?
DIZZY DAVE: A very small mother?

How does Horrid Henry send funny messages?
By tee-hee mail.

HORRIBLE HISTORY HOWLERS

MISS BATTLE-AXE:
Where did Napoleon
keep his armies?
RUDE RALPH:
Up his sleevies?

LAZY LINDA:
I wish we lived in the olden days.
MISS BATTLE-AXE: Why?
LAZY LINDA: Then there wouldn't
be so much history to learn.

MISS BATTLE-AXE: During which
battle was Lord Nelson killed?
CLEVER CLARE: His last one!

MISS BATTLE-AXE: What came after the Stone Age and the Bronze Age?
GREEDY GRAHAM: The sausage!

MISS BATTLE-AXE: What's the difference between the death rate in Elizabethan times and the death rate nowadays?
CLEVER CLARE: It's still the same – one death per person.

MISS BATTLE-AXE: Who invented fractions?
MOODY MARGARET: Henry the Eighth.

Why do Egyptian pyramids have doorbells?
So you can toot-n-come in.

MISS BATTLE-AXE:
Who was the
fastest runner in
history?
AEROBIC AL:
Adam – because
he came first in
;the human race!

MISS BATTLE-AXE: Tell me
something important that didn't exist
100 years ago.
HORRID HENRY: Me!

MERRY MATHS

What's the fastest way to count cows?
Using a cowculator

MISS BATTLE-AXE: If you had
10p, and you asked your dad for another
10p, how much would you have?
ANXIOUS ANDREW: Er…
10p, Miss.
MISS BATTLE-AXE: You don't
know your arithmetic, Andrew!
ANXIOUS ANDREW: You don't
know my dad, Miss.

MISS BATTLE-AXE:
If you add 26 and
301, then double it
and divide by 6,
what do you get?
HORRID HENRY:
The wrong answer.

Why was the Maths book puzzled?
Because it had a lot of questions.

Why was the zero punished?
Because it was noughty.

MISS BATTLE-AXE: How can
you make so many mistakes in
one maths class?
SOUR SUSAN: Because I get
here early.

What kind of tree is good at Maths?
A geometry!

RIBTICKLING TESTS

HORRID HENRY: I don't think I deserved zero for this test.
MISS BATTLE-AXE: I don't either, but it's the lowest I can give.

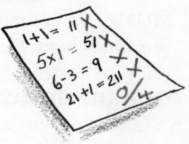

How did the dinosaur pass his exam?
With extinction.

DAD: Were your test results good?
HORRID HENRY: Yes and no.
DAD: What do you mean, "Yes and no"?
HORRID HENRY: YES, my test results were NO good.

BRAINY BRIAN: Let's have a race to say our tables.
CLEVER CLARE: *Our tables.* I win!

MUM: All your teachers have given you a bad report, Henry. What have you been doing?
HORRID HENRY: Nothing, Mum.

DRACULA'S SCHOOL REPORT
Reading: *better in the dark*
Writing: *upside down*
Cricket: *shows promise as a bat*

HALLOWEEN CACKLES

What do birds say at Halloween?
Trick or tweet!

Why do witches all look the same?
So you can't tell which witch is which.

What kind of monster has the best hearing?
The eeriest!

*Did you hear about the vampire
who needed a drink?*
He was bloodthirsty.

Knock, knock!
Who's there?
Ivan.
Ivan who?
Ivan to suck your blood!

Why do vampires like thick books?
They like stories they can really get their teeth into.

What goes "Flap, flap! Bite, bite! Ouch, ouch!"
Dracula with toothache.

What do you call a witch's garage?
A broom cupboard.

What was the name of the little witch's brother?
He was cauld-Ron.

How many witches does it take to change a light bulb?
Only one, but she changes it into a toad.

GHOSTLY GIGGLES

What did the mother ghost say to the naughty baby ghost?
Don't spook until you're spooken to.

What do you get if you cross a ghost with a packet of crisps?
Snacks that go crunch in the night.

Why can't ghosts tell fibs?
Because you can see right through them.

What do you get if you cross a footballer with a ghost?
A ghoulie.

Horrid Henry went to a Halloween party
with a sheet on his head.
"Are you a ghost?" asked Rude Ralph.
"No, I'm an unmade bed."

What's a baby ghost's favourite game?
Peek-a-BOO!

*Why was the bowl
of soup so scary?*
It was scream
of tomato.

How do monsters count to twenty-three?
On their fingers.

DIZZY DAVE: My bike's haunted.
HORRID HENRY: How do you know?
DIZZY DAVE: Because it's got spooks
on the wheels.

KNOCK, KNOCK! WINTER'S COMING

Knock, knock!
Who's there?
Worm.
Worm who?
Worm in there,
but cold outside.

Knock, knock!
Who's there?
Aunt.
Aunt who?
Aunt these jokes terrible.

Knock, knock!
Who's there?
Nana.
Nana who?
Nana your business.

Knock, knock!
Who's there?
Olivia.
Olivia who?
Olivia, but I've lost my key

Knock, knock!
Who's there?
Beezer.
Beezer who?
Beezer black and yellow.

Knock, knock!
Who's there?
Mickey.
Mickey who?
Mickey won't fit, that's why I'm knocking.

Knock, knock!
Who's there?
Snow.
Snow who?
Snow use, I've forgotten my keys.

WINTER

I LOVE winter! Snowballs and weather so cold and wet and miserable there's no way Mum and Dad  can drag me on nature walks so I get to stay warm and snug on the sofa watching telly! And of course winter means ... Christmas! Don't let Santa get away with not giving you all those great presents you deserve – especially those Bugle Blast Boots he forgot last year. And remember to make loads of noise on New Year's Eve!

WINTRY WHEEZES

What did one snowman say to the other?
"Can you smell carrots?"

*What do you call a snowman
on a sunny day?*
A puddle.

*What food do you get when you cross a
snowman with a polar bear?*
A brrr–grrr.

*How do you know when there's
a snowman in your bed?*
You wake up wet!

*What do you get if you cross
a snowman and a shark?*
Frost bite!

Why don't mountains get cold in the winter?
Because they wear snow caps.

*What goes: Now you see me, now you
don't, now you see me, now you don't?*
A snowman on a zebra crossing.

What sort of ball doesn't bounce?
A snowball.

CHILLY CHUCKLES

What's white, furry and smells minty?
A polo bear.

How do sheep keep warm in the winter?
They turn on the central bleating.

*What animal would you get if you
tied ice cubes around your neck?*
A chin chiller.

*What do you call
a polar bear in
a jungle?*
Lost!

How does Jack Frost travel about?
On his icicle.

*What do you get if you cross
a goldfish and an ice cube?*
A cold fish.

Why are igloos round?
So polar bears can't hide in the corners.

What falls in winter but doesn't get hurt?
Snow.

Why shouldn't you ice skate on a full stomach?
Because it's easier on an ice rink.

JOLLY
CHRISTMAS JESTS

BRAINY BRIAN: What's the difference between an elephant and a postbox?

BEEFY BERT: I dunno.
BRAINY BRIAN: Well, I'm not asking you to post my Christmas cards.

What did the big cracker say to the little cracker?
My pop is bigger than yours.

What did one angel say to the other?
Halo there.

What do angry mice send to each other
at Christmas?
Cross mouse cards.

What happened to the
thief who stole a
Christmas calendar?
He got 12 months!

What did Adam say on
the day before Christmas?
It's Christmas, Eve!

Knock, knock!
Who's there?
Holly.
Holly who?
Holly-days are here again.

Why is it always cold at Christmas?
Because it's Decembrrrrrr!

*What's the difference between the ordinary
alphabet and the Christmas alphabet?*
The Christmas alphabet has No-el.

*What is green, covered with tinsel
and goes ribbet ribbet?*
Mistle-toad!

Why are Christmas trees like bad knitters?
They both drop their needles!

FUNNY FOOD

PERFECT PETER: Can I have a
canary for Christmas?
MUM: No, you can have turkey
like the rest of us.

*Who is never
hungry at
Christmas?*
The turkey –
he's always
stuffed.

whewwww

*How does good King Wenceslas
like his pizzas?*
Deep pan, crisp and even.

What do you get if you cross a Christmas tree with an apple?
A pine-apple.

What do snowmen like for lunch?
Icebergers.

We had grandma for Christmas dinner.
Really, we had turkey!

What's the definition of a balanced diet?
A Christmas cake in each hand.

COMICAL CAROLS

What do elephants sing at Christmas?
No-elephants, No-elephants…

How do sheep greet each other at Christmas?
A merry Christmas to ewe.

What's Tarzan's favourite Christmas song?
Jungle Bells.

*What do they sing in the desert
at Christmas time?*
"Oh camel ye
faithful…"

*What Christmas carol
do Horrid Henry's
parents like?*
Silent night.

What's a gorilla's favourite
Christmas song?
King Kong
merrily
on high.

What did the guests sing
at Father Christmas's party?
Freeze a jolly good fellow!

What's a hairdresser's favourite
Christmas song?
Oh, comb all ye faithful.

What musical instrument was the fisherman
given for Christmas?
A cast–a–net.

Knock, knock!
Who's there?
Wayne.
Wayne who?
(Sing) "Wayne in a manger, no crib for a bed."

96

SANTA SNIGGERS

What is Father Christmas's wife called?
Mary Christmas.

Who delivers the cat's Christmas presents?
Santa Paws.

Why does Father Christmas go down the chimney?
Because it soots him.

How many chimneys does Father Christmas go down on Christmas Eve?
Stacks!

Why is it difficult to keep a secret at the North Pole?
Because your teeth chatter.

Why does Santa like to work in the garden?
Because he likes to hoe hoe hoe.

Why does Santa wear bright red braces?
To hold his trousers up.

What does a cat on the beach have in common with Christmas?
Sandy claws.

What type of cars do Santa's elves drive?
TOY-otas.

What do elves learn at school?
The Elf-abet.

How do elves get tummy ache?
By goblin their food.

What does Santa do when his elves are naughty?
He gives them the sack.

Who looks after Father Christmas when he's ill?
The National Elf Service.

REINDEER RIBTICKLERS

What do you call
a reindeer wearing
ear muffs?
Anything you
want because he
can't hear you!

What you call a reindeer with only three legs?
Eileen.

What do you call a reindeer with only one eye?
No idea.

What do you call a reindeer with
no legs and only one eye?
Still no idea.

Where would you find a reindeer with no legs?
Where you left it.

What reindeer can jump higher than a house?
All of them – a house can't jump.

How do you get milk
from a reindeer?
Rob its fridge
and run like mad.

Why do reindeer scratch themselves?
Because no one else knows where
they itch!

Why do reindeers wear fur coats?
Because they'd look silly in plastic macs.

KNOCK, KNOCK! LET THE NEW YEAR IN

Knock, knock!
Who's there?
Luke.
Luke who?
*Luke through the
window and you'll see.*

    Knock, knock!
    Who's there?
    Howard.
    Howard who?
    *Howard you like it if I made
    you stand out in the cold?*

Knock, knock!
Who's there?
Doris.
Doris who?
Doris closed, that's why I'm knocking.

Knock, knock!
Who's there?
Harry.
Harry who?
Harry up and open the door.

Knock, knock!
Who's there?
Police.
Police who?
Police open the door.

Knock, knock!
Who's there?
Police.
Police who?
*POLICE STOP TELLING THESE
AWFUL KNOCK, KNOCK JOKES!*

Well, that's it, guys. I am out of jokes. Lucky for me I got 365, that's 'cause I am the best, most amazing and totally brilliant...

Actually you only have 364 jokes, Henry.

Liar!

I counted, Henry. It's only 364.

Out of my way, worm!
You're wrong, you
wormy worm toad,
I've counted them
too, watch, 362 ...
363 ... 364 ... 364...
Ooops.

Okay, listen up, everyone.
I need one more great joke.
Help me out!!!!

Send your absolute best joke to

Horrid Henry's
Joke Search
c/o Orion Children's Books,
5 Upper St Martin's Lane,
London WC2H 9EA.

Horrid Henry will print his favourite
joke in the next brilliant joke book!

HORRID HENRY BOOKS

Horrid Henry
Horrid Henry and the Secret Club
Horrid Henry Tricks the Tooth Fairy
Horrid Henry's Nits
Horrid Henry Gets Rich Quick
Horrid Henry's Haunted House
Horrid Henry and the Mummy's Curse
Horrid Henry's Revenge
Horrid Henry and the
  Bogey Babysitter
Horrid Henry's Stinkbomb

Horrid Henry's Underpants
Horrid Henry Meets the Queen
Horrid Henry and the Mega-Mean
  Time Machine
Horrid Henry and the Football Fiend
Horrid Henry's Christmas Cracker
Horrid Henry's Christmas Cracker
Horrid Henry and the Abominable
  Snowman
Horrid Henry Robs the Bank
Horrid Henry Wakes the Dead

Early Readers

Don't Be Horrid, Henry!
Horrid Henry's Birthday Party
Horrid Henry's Holiday

Horrid Henry's Underpants
Horrid Henry Gets Rich Quick

Colour Books

Horrid Henry's Big Bad Book
Horrid Henry's Wicked Ways
Horrid Henry's Evil Enemies

Horrid Henry Rules the World
Horrid Henry's House of Horrors
Horrid Henry's Dreadful Deeds

Joke Books

Horrid Henry's Joke Book
Horrid Henry's Jolly Joke Book

Horrid Henry's Might Joke Book
Horrid Henry versus Moody Margaret

Activity Books

Horrid Henry's Brainbusters
Horrid Henry's Headscratchers
Horrid Henry's Mindbenders
Horrid Henry's Colouring Book
Horrid Henry's Puzzle Book

Horrid Henry's Sticker Book
Horrid Henry's Classroom Chaos
Horrid Henry's Holiday Havoc
Horrid Henry Runs Riot
Horrid Henry's Annual 2010